2,99

THE DOG OF MEMORY

Helen Farish was born in Cumbria in 1962. She studied for her undergraduate degree at Durham University, and completed an MA and PhD at Oxford Brookes University. Her doctoral thesis explored the work of Sharon Olds and Louise Glück. She lectured in English Literature and Creative Writing at Sheffield Hallam University and Lancaster University. She was also a Visiting Scholar at the University of New Hampshire for six months and a Visiting Lecturer at Sewanee University, Tennessee. She has been a Fellow at Hawthornden International Centre for Writers and received residences at the Fundación Valparaiso in Spain and the International Centre for Writers and Translators in Rhodes. In 2004-05 she was Poet in Residence at the Wordsworth Trust, Grasmere. She now lives in Cumbria and can be contacted via her website, helenfarish.co.uk.

Her debut collection, *Intimates* (Cape, 2005), a Poetry Book Society Recommendation, was shortlisted for the T.S. Eliot Prize and won the Forward Prize for Best First Collection. Her poems have been broadcast on BBC Radio 3, and an audio CD, *Helen Farish reading from her poems*, was released by the Poetry Archive in 2009. Her collections, *Nocturnes at Nohant: The decade of Chopin and Sand* (2012) and *The Dog of Memory* (2016) are both published by Bloodaxe Books.

HELEN FARISH

The Dog of Memory

BLOODAXE BOOKS

ISBN: 978 1 78037 318 8

First published 2016 by
Bloodaxe Books Ltd,
Eastburn,
South Park,
Hexham,
Northumberland NE46 1BS.

www.bloodaxebooks.com
For further information about Bloodaxe titles
please visit our website or write to
the above address for a catalogue.

Supported using public funding by
**ARTS COUNCIL
ENGLAND**

Cover design: Neil Astley & Pamela Robertson-Pearce.

Printed in Great Britain by Bell & Bain Limited, Glasgow, Scotland, on
acid-free paper sourced from mills with FSC chain of custody certification.

for Margaret Maxwell

ACKNOWLEDGEMENTS

Acknowledgements are due to the editors of the following publications where some of these poems first appeared: *Branch-Lines: Edward Thomas and Contemporary Poetry* (Enitharmon Press, 2007), *Crrritic* (Sussex Academic Press, 2011), *English, The Fire Crane, In Your Own Time: The Northern Poetry Workshop Anthology* (Shoestring Press, 2012), *Life Writing, The London Review of Books, Matter, The Moth, Mslexia, Oxford Magazine, PN Review, Poetry London, Poetry News, The Poetry Review, South Bank Poetry, The Spectator, The Times Literary Supplement*, and *A Winter Garland* (Wordsworth Trust, 2006).

Earlier versions of 'Fallen apple tree' and 'Judgement Day' were published on www.blinking-eye.co.uk and www.diamondtwig.co.uk.

'Missing the rain' (inspired by Tess Gallagher's essay, 'My Father's Love Letters') and 'Storm, Bavaria' (inspired by 'Waiting for the Storm' by Gerald Mangan) were written for *The Poetics of the Archive* (Bloodaxe Books/Newcastle University, 2015).

My thanks to the Northern Poetry Workshop for all the convivial and enlightening evenings during which many of these poems had their first reading. And warm thanks to my dear friends, Bernard O'Donoghue and Steven Matthews, for their readings of the manuscript.

My gratitude to Jane Cook for all her support.

CONTENTS

I

May I always remember when
We drank our wine as darkness died

HAFEZ

A borrowing

Over time my memory relocated us
to Palace Green. Perhaps it required
a dramatic backdrop, the open air
the library's Short Loan desk lacked.
You wore a striped blazer in an ironic way.
I wore a long black dress, though it was spring
and the night that lay ahead perfumed
by the freesias you bought as we walked
up Claypath, you on short loan, something
my memory is powerless to change
except by not returning you.

My Casablanca

He threw me in the air and said
What a brilliant idea! I loved being
an idea, like all ideas weightless,
and therefore easy to throw
into the air hanging about
the door to his apartment.

I wonder where I got the courage
to cross the city and surprise him,
why I wasn't like my mother waiting
for a partner at the dance?
I've never been very content
to hang about, but I could have stayed
(brilliant) in the air
he threw me into forever.

Allington Cross

I keep thinking how we wait all year
and possibly longer (because not every summer
contains such days) for such days.

Because when summer is at its height
its poise is the pause of a church bell suspended
rim-up after its stroke, mouth open.

At Allington Cross the whole landscape
was a bell mouth open, *ah*, the luminous
untrammelled now of it, rim-up and poised.

And paused at the crossroads in the liquefying
high-sky heat, I thought of the composer
who cycled round and round the square
so as not to miss a note of the broadcast symphony.

Palermo, *da capo*

The four minutes of this love theme expand
to cover nineteen eighty-eight – a phrase
for winter, summer, a minim per month,
quavers for each morning we swung open
the sun-anointed shutters, and a sweet pause
for the sugar seller's song below – *Zucchero!*

But life is live, as with this performance,
and no one filmed us walking down Via Roma,
no one recorded how the woman prayed
for grace on the steps of the Gesù, no one
framed in black and white our taxi climbing
Salita Raffadali on a one-way fare.
There would have been a bowl of lemons,
a curtain's cinematic flap somewhere.

Missing the rain

Grass the colour of a worn teddy bear
makes her long for rain, for spongy air.

Rain and poetry are a spark and its flame,
roots and a tree. But the ground is hard

as a hardback in Arizona
where she can neither bury nor plant.

The train in her recurring dream breaks
down in the desert, days from Port Angeles.

Waking to conditioned air, she plays a CD
of rain which isn't, of course, the same

as the faithful grey-green rain of home
holding quiet faces at wood-framed windows.

What did geography teach about the rain?
She learnt the names of the current, the strait,

the mountains, but then found a poem
in which rain only falls when the earth

is meditating, and the earth loves
to meditate in Washington State,

Port Angeles, the peninsula town,
with its low lichen-coloured light.

Stuck in Tucson with an essay to write,
it's too hot to think until late. Influence?

She cites early reading, a particular name,
then crosses it out, pauses, writes *rain*.

Jane Eyre, a sequel

1 *From Ferndean to Villa Céline*

Reader, don't assume that once we married
Ferndean remained our home, with its grass-plat
in place of flower-beds, narrow latticed windows,
trees ranked closer than in a Gothic dream.
Edward let slip one day in June when the rain
was small but penetrating how he owned
a white-washed villa, bougainvillea-draped,
its windows beguiled by the permissive sea.
I pictured myself on the terrace filling bowls
with misshapen lemons, bunching lavender,
sketching al fresco in loose cream linens –
my black beaver bonnet and matching muff,
my merino cloak all stuffed into a chest:
moth-fodder. We were off within the week.

2 *Edward asks Jane what she recalls of Gateshead, her first home*

A red room. Bewick's *History of Birds* flying
towards my brow. And a china plate,
not thrown but placed on my knee by Bessie.
I ate the tart impatient to come eye to eye
with the bird of paradise whose plumage
I'd recognised – yolk yellow with the red
of congealed blood. At its throat, emerald.
All crumbs removed, it eyed me like a gypsy
holding a palm. 'I'd give something to see
this fortune-telling china plate,' Edward said,
and since I could neither show him the original
nor improve his limited vision, I painted
my childhood memory onto china.

Peaches ripen at the door to my studio
and those early plates are now collectible.
But in my new work there's an old-fashioned girl
who wears a winter bonnet. She sits on a stile,
hands hidden in a muff, her merino cloak
muddied at the hem, and in the background
the ruins of a hall, paneless windows, arches
forced apart, a rookery, and snow, fast-falling,
ushered in by the wind and requiring only
the withdrawal of my black-tipped brush.

3 *Jane's dream*

Last night I dreamt I went to Yorkshire again,
a curious place to dream of as I slept
beside the tideless sea of the south.

I must have taken the old road to the house
and at hay-time, hedges pinned with roses,
cloud like lace on a dress-maker's floor.

With Edward's permission, a blonde woman
was removing pictures from where they hung
on Thornfield's walls, pictures I'd painted.

I could see my iceberg, in the foreground a head,
a woman's, with fixed, glassy eyes and a brow
so bloodless it merged with the Polar sky.

And there, above an ugly sea, my cormorant,
in its beak a gold ring, and on the water below
an arm, a woman's, wax-white, out-stretched.

Edward (when first in love) had framed the contents
of my sketchbook. Now he stood by, silent,
his mistress saying of each one, *brutta, brutta!*

Waking saved me from killing her, but I snapped
at Edward as he moved towards me in bed.
I was having an idea for a painting, seeing red.

4 *Jane and her son mourn Edward*

The story young Edward liked best
on those September days when we stumbled
round the house surprised

by furniture, fumbling for cutlery to spear food
we had no desire to eat, closing shutters
against the sun which had no business to rise –

was the one about his father seeing colours:
the gold of the watch chain round my neck
and the Riviera blue of my smock.

When the list grew – olive green, apricot –
we left Villa Céline, sailed to Dover,
then a carriage through the rain to London,

a Mr Lake, who swept aside all his patients
in order to see Edward Fairfax Rochester
to whom he said, with a twinkle in his eye

and a glance at my figure, that the colour
of our son's eyes – blue or brown –
would not be lost on his father.

The irony, then, that our son's eyes
were black, deep-water-of-the-north black,
with flashes of silver I alone saw.

A pet of her own was what she needed.
The masterful men in her life had dogs,
wolfhounds the length of hearths – Pilot, Carlo –
who took sides when the men were in a mood.
But let's think back to Jane's childhood –
if she picked up a book it was taken from her
to become a missile, her blood on its spine;
if she drew the pictures her imagination supplied,
the paper, the pencils, weren't hers; even the fire
had to disobey its owner to warm her.

She saw me for sale in a shop window.
Middle-aged, she stood letting her eyes fill.
Perhaps a recent death or that opaque
longing which seizes her sometimes
during a moment's stillness in a public place.
Or an early memory – finding a litter
of white kittens in a hay loft, secretly
adopting the smallest till a stable lad
spied on her one morning.

From behind glass tabbied with rain,
I tracked her, across the street, the square,
where she looked back as though
fearing she'd see again that squirming sack.

Underground city

As I read I convince myself
I remember it, that road trip, the lake
passed on the way, yes the lake,
and the underground city, Kaymakli,
from which I emerged to find the sky
a colour I call *unforgettable* –
an experience of red.

In the sunset, two things move –
smoke, an obedient line
from every square white house,
and a woman, unseeing,
in a ghostly white headdress.
Once upon a time I stood there
in her world and she walked past.

The dog itself

Memory rounds this up, breathless,
like the dog herding sheep
below the bedroom window:

dropped at my feet are smells –
wool in the rain, my aunt's
cigarette smoked on the hoof,

gorse also, firs making green
(and what it all means,
that too has a smell).

Not forgetting the dog itself,
so pleased with its work,
I must pen it in quick.

Pancake Day

(for Bobby)

We must have been there once on Pancake Day
because I'm not inventing it, the plate
of pancakes brought from the flagged kitchen
and set down: the welly-boot-high pile

one of the seven wonders of being
aged eight when it was only natural
for nothing to be finite. That the height
of the pile must have lowered is a fact;

likewise that there would have been lemons
squeezed, empty plates, hot-lard smoke
in the air. But my memory is greedy
and will not share the feast it has found –

it's the difference between the pancakes
and the scene I've built around them
that tells me only they are true.
And nothing, not even this, can make them lie.

De Bottelier, Bruges

(for Karen)

We are dining like merchants
with velvet purses, Baltic furs

at the nape of our necks
as we muse on the spent day.

On the wall, a still life
of Castilian oranges and lemons.

Outside the window, the canal
is bottle-brown, amber light

on the stone bridge, a sky
of darkest felt, and a nun,

business-like, in a spice-
coloured robe. My friend,

into what shape should we cut
tomorrow's unwoven cloth?

L'homme tranquille

81 rue des Martyrs, Paris

Diners have written poems on napkins,
pinned them to *Gauloises Blondes* walls
next to film and theatre posters for shows

whose run is over. A ceiling fan
is reluctant to disturb the heat slumped
after a hard day in the city.

We watch the owner smooth cloths
and make precise adjustments to cutlery.
He charms the querulous family,

the couple at the bar, and if we ever return,
you and I, he'll shake our hands,
test you on the winning score.

And what I'll order will be time
to pin a poem to a napkin
before the curtain falls.

Pastoral

How does Casterbridge appear from the air
on this coppery evening, the mayor having dined,
the clock sounding eight, emptying the square?

Stone of as many greys as tree bark
has browns, or like the fur of a hare,
grey and brown mixed. And as the bird arcs

higher, it sees how compact is this box
of chimneys, roofs, certain windows earmarked
to be rubied by the sun, church towers whose flocks

of pigeons grow sleepy. Acres of coomb,
cornland and down display the orthodox
gold and green of the season, but it's the blooms

of the town's back gardens which delight
the bee who uses them as his stockroom.
Like a merchant with the feel of samite

lingering on finger and thumb, the satisfied
bee sashays through a town as much his birthright
as the surrounding meads, so countrified

is Casterbridge. But to choose between the bird
and the bee, wait for Allhallowtide
and the southerly storms which leave the air furred

like the velvet of a rose – refined –
and which the dozing bee misses, while the bird
treats the sky like a page it has signed.

Elizabeth and Darcy go walking out

There can be no Elizabeth and Darcy tourist trail.
Happiness takes them off the map. Even their author
doesn't follow though it's she who's made them

so happy they wander miles without knowing
quite where. But to pose a prosaic question –
Lizzy and Darcy set off from Longbourn, a place

Lizzy has always walked, so how is it she's 'beyond
her own knowledge' of the church gates and copses,
cottage doors and meadows they wander past?

Sleepy reds being deepened, flame yellows lifted,
air gentled to hold still the suddenly elegiac robin;
the autumnal harvest of the day and which way taken

at the fork in the spinney – all this the pair fail
to notice; neither can they look the other in the eye.
Waiting by the hornbeam hedge of home, their author

sees the darkening sky. Was it hard in that chapter
not to follow, not to have her share? Three times
she tells us the lovers wander without knowing where.

Storm, Bavaria

Grass dried to bronze fur. The plushy air
of summer thunder seducing
the foothills. A Mitteleuropean wind
preceding rain. Here it comes.
The first drops are transparent capitals
in a text seconds from being scrambled.

And if in memory it is legible –
that fluid moment, the downhill run
on a path so bendy as if the wind
had thrown it in the air and let it fall –
should we be grateful for the top copy,
the polished version, or lament the lost drafts?

Athens

Did you take me for a Greek word?
Most do, but I pre-date the Greeks.

I used to describe a limestone plateau
where dusty snakes and small owls lived

with a people from whose mouths emerged
my extensive family. I miss the sound

of my original kin as I muck in
with this new crowd, biting my tongue

when I hear two or even three words stuck
together to describe skies my first family

got in a syllable – skies that occur at nightfall
in Attica after days of languor in late August

(you know the ones). But as I mourn the fall
in standards, I tell myself to be grateful

I'm uttered without nostalgia and remain
the name of this place. I'd hate to join Siam,

Byzantium, Saigon, Rangoon, Bombay –
beautiful words in various stages of decay.

A goddess, a city and a tree

Known for her strength,
Athena can throw
a spear like a dart,

and on the day
of the contest for Athens
it's a bull's eye –

not just Attica's
but the world's first olive tree
springs where her spear falls.

Athena is surprised
how at ease the tree is,
the Saronic Gulf

merely its backyard, the slopes
of the Akropolis simply a source
of afternoon shade.

Athena's competitor packs his bag,
the fruit of the new tree
glossy as his lost dream.

On Philopappos hill – lizards
seeing blindly into the distance,
empty olive oil cans

already being planted
with geraniums in the city below –
Athena throws her spear again

through air she may as well begin polluting.
A chair appears, a table,
a bowl of olives, an ashtray.

She reaches into the back pocket
of her jeans, sits down,
lights up.

II

We look at the world once, in childhood.
The rest is memory.

LOUISE GLÜCK

Calling

Lass gives me a home,
a geographic location,

an ordnance survey
grid reference.

I hear my Dad,
Oh lass.

Judgement Day

Michelangelo requested that his body be buried in
Santa Croce so that on Judgement Day the first thing
he'd see would be Brunelleschi's cathedral dome.

I'd be under the apple tree
not far from the daffodils
which every spring spell ANNE.

Dad cutting the grass
would be the first thing I'd see.
Don't die again, the first thing I'd say.

Somehow it became everything –
the cobblestone house, the barn,
the yard like a stage,

the ghyll view, clothes drying in winds
which had names, and the sycamores
I called Father, Son and Holy Ghost.

And each day we laid innocently
on top of the last dug our names deeper.
Spring will always bring them back

in the distance between the Keswick apple
and the back door, the slight incline,
the lilac, the old swing swinging

as though I'd just jumped off,
aged ten, my whole life
behind me.

Tea-time at my aunt's

Snow, like memory, made the monkey clock's tick
louder, muffling wheels on the lonning, footsteps
crossing the yard. The monkey puffed up his chest,
adjusted his bow tie and waited eagerly
for the hand that would be waved like a wand
over his long pendulum, bringing out
the gleam.
              What is it that you mean with all this
talk of clocks coming to life?

There was a novelty clock, a snowy afternoon.
Look closer – there's a child who doesn't know
to say to the snow, the afternoon, the ticking clock,
Please don't go. She's pouring tea into milk
(a novelty) and eyeing up the last piece
of krispie cake she knows she'll have to share.
Of this room, in later life, she'll make an everywhere.

In deep

What if everyone who ever lived and died here had left
one thing behind, one thing to be preserved for as long
as the four walls stand?

I'll approach Death myself, get my face known
so when he comes round to the idea
and sees he needs a curator
for this unique museum,
he'll find me as I am tonight, resigned
to the snow cutting me off
(for hours it's been falling).

I'll be given a piece of paper to sign.
I might feel important, excited –
Of all the people who've ever lived out their lives here...

Yes, he'll say, except the museum will open with you:
the first donation will be yours
and yours the ghost receiving it.
And no, it has to be something that can be held.

What to do, then, with the white magic of this undark night?

Cahier

In the *John Menzies* A6 notebook
in which my father mirrored
French with English

and studied equations, the foreign
codes of his profession, I copy
the writing on the byre beams:

May 10th 1945 white cow bulled
has a line through it.
The following year there are dates

for the light cow, the dark, the heifer.
What happened on *2nd July 1947* is lost.
On *25th July* something was *Late*.

There's no evidence that a noose
was found a few beams away
a decade further on, pale calves

bawling all night. But the story I heard
makes it hard to copy those *l*'s,
the exaggerated loops of the farmer

whose pencil-on-wood logbook
has become his animal plea,
his *J'étais ici*, his don't-cross-out-me.

La Pergola du Parc, Casablanca

If only we could say to death
what we said to that little man

who came uninvited to our table,
ordered a drink and told the waiter

we'd be paying. 'It's on their tab,'
he said in a language he thought

we'd not understand. So I said
to the *petit homme, Allez-vous-en* –

and the park was ours again,
trees with upside-down flowers,

the café's tinkling water feature.
If only we could say to death

Allez-vous-en, ignore his parting leer,
get back to where we were.

Rough Guide to Vienna

Fifteen things not to miss: the Opera,
museums, parks, the rich, *Kaffeehäuser*,
'The Third Man', tram 1, tram 2 (for the view),
Freud escaping, his sisters not, hanged Jews
(gold effigies) on nineteenth-century
watch chains, shopkeepers finding graffiti
promising a holiday in Dachau,
a cartoon of Jews eating grass like cows
on the Prater, women scrubbing the streets
being urinated on by SS
(this considered a treat by onlookers),
Berggasse – birthplace of the unconscious:
'At a party, I looked down (in the dream)
and saw brown fur where my heart should have been.'

The death of Doctor Zhivago

Why have him die in August
on the hot cobbles of Presnya street
after an epic volume of snow? It snows
in chapter one on his mother's grave.
In chapter two when a Moscow door
admits guests the air rushes past
flickering with metallic sparks of snow;
inside the supper table is white,
the bottles frosted. In chapter three
the snow is remembered, not actual
(a dying woman says of childhood
in the Urals, *And the snow, the snow!*
Higher than the roofs!). Watching its boats
being hauled to the backyards of Yuryatin,
the river smells the snow on its way
to chapter four. In chapter six
Alexander Alexandrovich hunts
for his second snow boot: it's the first
blizzard of the winter and the third
winter of the war; at a crossroads
Zhivago struggles to read the print
of the late extra, its black and white
obscured by the gunfire-grey snow.
And the empty windows of home –
how poignant when looked in on
by the street which will never see
this fur-clad family again.
Polka dots of snow, snow large
and woolly or a curtain of the stuff
descending as resolutely as if
calling a sudden halt to a play:
how the snow piles up in chapter seven!

That train leaving Moscow for the east –
its passengers will find themselves
for three days, shovels in hand,
the villagers all fled or dead, the sun
slipping the cold shadow of a birch
through the window of the ruined station,
unseen. So much snow has to thaw
and that takes care of chapter eight.
In chapter nine the snow is falling
in the doctor's diary and in the pages
of *War and Peace*, of Pushkin being read
in the fairytale house in the forest;
imagine the fastness and the great
unending white of the plains patterned
by hares. Winter is the time to write.
White is limited in the next chapter
to roofs, snow like rock refusing to melt
while below roads wetten and blacken.
Violet-mauve takes over, the colour of lilac
in bud, sweets in jars, and memory
(the lavender twilight of a shop interior,
the tea-leaf sweepings of yesterday –
a lifetime's fragments vanishing
on the stained cobbles of a street
in a city so changed its inhabitants
struggle to find their way home).
In chapter eleven there's a ground frost
on which a kingdom of snow settles
in chapter twelve like death, turning
the Whites, the Reds, the partisans
to felt-booted ghosts. Observe Zhivago
eating snow then skiing all the way
to chapter thirteen, arriving in spring
with a heart condition which gives him
two and a half chapters to live.

Summer is over in six words. The Muses,
poor things, their lyres and cymbals silent,
dream of fragrant Arkadia as snow performs
its artistry on their marble figures, blinding
eyes which have been watching the doctor
and his nurse in the house opposite;
imagine one of these stone beauties,
the one in love with poetry, climbing
down from the top floor, finding
a sleigh to follow the doctor poet
across chapter fourteen's pale blue
moonlit wilderness to Varykino:
finally a writing desk, lamplight
of dim gold, finally time! Real wolves,
a row of them with ink-black shadows
coming closer each night, cannot scare
Zhivago, only what they represent:
a plot to separate him from everything
he has loved and conclude with him circled
by onlookers who soon leave the scene –
the boredom of a natural death combined
with August heat, plum-dark thunder.
If he'd fallen in new-page snow,
the best background for drops of blood
artfully arranged in a line...
But he collapses on cobbles and is gone,
denied a final return to chapter five.
What would he have remembered
of its days? Lime-tree blossom
in the centuries-old garden of a Countess,
a woman ironing in a pantry telling him
he'd forget, the might of the Russian spring
rolling up and over the house like a wave,
that cow bawling its grief to the stars.

HMS *Affray*

Your posting – at the last minute
it was changed, so your name
wasn't with the lists of the dead
when *Affray*'s catastrophe
made front-page news.
Ahead of you lay forty more years.
But small-print woe
can be as effective in the end,
can take you to the bottom
the same as a naval exercise
gone wrong. In the surgery,
is it your own doctor or a locum
who says, *Here is the hat,*
here is your name?

Cavafy's suitcase

He was leaving like one long prepared,
like a brave man, until he saw the suitcase.

Pulled from his closet by one of those friends
the lonely pray for, it was hospital-sized.

She would return alone to close
the balcony shutters, to spare him that;

below, a little movement in the street, the shops,
the brothel open, the gardens of the Greek hospital

composed of the deep green gleams of palms
and blossom the white of Christening Bibles.

He was leaving the second floor flat,
its Byzantine clutter, red and mauve rooms,

like one long prepared, like a brave man,
until he saw the suitcase: it was the memory

of its purchase, that leather shop
in rue de l'Hôpital Grec, dabbing light sweat

from his brow, long ago, a young man
waiting for him in Cairo.

Moon x 6

A re-reading of Tennyson's 'Morte d'Arthur'

I remembered the moon, but I'd have said
we hear about it once, then are trusted
to read the whole poem moonlit –

the 'dark strait' we imagine night-bright,
we supply a wave-broken stripe of moon
on sea and lake, and we enlarge all sound.

But the moon works hard in this poem.
Without the second moon, Sir Bedivere
could not have found his way to the lake,

and having guided him to where he must fling
Arthur's sword, the weapon's diamonds
(in the light of a third moon) outglitter a crown.

The knight questions why it should be drowned.
But once the sword is lake-spinning, a sudden
fourth moon ends Bedivere's doubt.

By contrast, how soft the sixth, gazing with grief
on Arthur's blood-matted curls. And the fifth?
The fifth is the only one I remember

from that sunny school room long ago:
I'm about to put my hand in the mythic air,
open my mouth and say, 'Moon, Sir?'

Cumberland, 1974

At my school debate
on the Anglo-Saxon word
versus 'Cumbria',
I argue for the old,
the one that belongs
with *hoolet*, *clarty*, *slape*,
with dark that is 'black dark',
with door snecks and byres
and a beyond that is
'the back of beyond'.

When I lose the argument,
I don't know that the soil
will continue its black-dark business,
or that the holly's foothold
in the high rock will remain
until King Arthur sets sail again.

Twelfth Night: or, What You Will

It was children, tucked in a footnote, playing
cherry-pit. I imagined Will, eyes lifting
to the open window. Carts heaped with cherries
(Merton Glory, Early Rivers) from orchards
in Kent, sound of water sluicing the street,
and the voices which had caused him to drift –
children's. Eating cherries just for the stones,
it's the first to get ten in the hole who wins.
Sir Toby gets a line (Act III, Scene IV)
and the girls and boys play till one becomes bored.
Suns set and children join the stones in the earth,
and of the orchards there remains a sixtieth.
As for school, for me what sticks is *Like a burr,*
Sir – this, for some reason, hasn't blurred.

Shift

When I was a child,
if my father

had an evening shift,
my mother was home,

and vice versa –
one or the other, not both,

never both
on the same shift.

Winter toad

I was reluctant to move the toad.
He thought he'd found the perfect bed –
the sawdust of years, cobwebbed logs,
camouflage so effective he was within
a hair's breadth of my foot.

In the furthest corner of the barn
where the floor is earth, my father
dug a pit he'd climb into, leaving me
a choice – step around it or follow,
camouflaged by love.

Still life

A Morris Minor covered in sheets dreams
of the road, birds' nests high up on beams
give rain and earth a surprising afterlife,
the kist, an unhinged gate, coal, a lost knife
in a drawer you can't find, woodworms, a pit,
one dart far from the bull's eye, spirit
bottled and otherwise, a tube of *No-Crode*
saying 'the more fool you' (off the record),
Elizabeth the First when young, a phone,
the wings of butterflies which flew their owners
through the fatal maw of the barn doors.
And the fifties pram, its *esprit de corps*
unwavering despite it all – the moths,
the emptiness, the lack of little coughs.

The Market Gardener's Tale, 1953

1 *The double-barrelled shotgun*

It's the third day after the fall:
a bad blow to the head as he hit

the barn floor. Nothing right
since the road accident in spring

when he'd been worrying –
a late frost, the plum blossom.

It's the third day after the fall:
another blow – prices low, a glut

of the crop he's been counting on.
His straw face at the upstairs window.

The shot sounds (a stooping woman
straightens) almost like the one before

and the one before that which flew
through the air simply to scare.

If anyone had picked that autumn's plums
the price per pound was fair.

2 *The spectacles*

On Tuesday Milburn's boy finds the glasses
on the barn floor, rims intact, a rope
over the beam above he'll never tire
talking of. It must have been a Tuesday
because John Fox the butcher drives
his white van with red lettering
up the lonning on a Friday,
and there were three days
between 'the fall' and what on no account
could be covered up as accidental.
Mr Fox happens to pull into the yard
an hour after the event, Dr Dolan there
for the second time that morning swearing
the patient at breakfast was not a man
about to do himself in. The butcher,
thinking they'll still need to eat,
carries meat through to the pantry –
ham and haslet, a pound of mince,
cuts of pork – then continues his round.
And Milburn's boy keeps the spectacles
he can put his fingers through,
without ever trying them on once
till the end of his born days.

3 *The marble*

Down by the old henhouse, the news
in last Friday's paper takes seconds
to curl up in the seedling flames.

The girls, two to a drawer, carry his things
from the unlit house to the bonfire,
passing rows of Little Marvel peas,

White Lisbon shallots, Cherry Belle radish
already bolting, strawberries
good for stewing or jam.

Everything about the place looks as though
it knows its fate, the wilderness
August will cultivate.

On one of the return legs, they hear
a rolling sound in the empty drawer –
a marble, bantam blue.

What you once owned

What if that suitcase came back,
the one you packed
for a year in a country
you'd not even visited?

What if that suitcase came back,
unopened? What if you hadn't lost,
thrown away, given away its contents,
things you believed you couldn't live without?

Woman, unfold the long black coat
which made you invisible on the winter streets
of that city, as if the first thing you threw away
was yourself.

The bus to Oualidia

(i.m. Denise Inge)

Further south, the bus stops at places maps dismiss:
a junction with a dirt road, a stray concrete hut,
a broken-down garage with a painterly pump –
places where those who will share the ride wait
never doubting that out of the intractable distance,
the dust ragged up by the Atlantic, the mystical
flame-orange sunset February is displaying
like the tail feathers of winter, their bus will come.

And along with the moustachioed men, the scarfed mothers,
there'll be foreigners, two young women on the right
half-way down, who'll need to be told they've arrived,
who'll be unaware as the door closes and they wait
for the bus to pull away – the man with the mint
still gusting its scent from the brush of their bags –
that they've just stepped down from a memory.

They drop off some details, pick up others,
keeping it on the road for twenty years,
the bus which never rusts.
I flag it down still, saving you a place.
Through the flame-orange dust,
your beautiful face.

Aftermath

Nine hundred camels took the toppled god
from where the earthquake had made
light work of the bronze sixty cubits high.
Saracens did the loading: generations
of islanders had refused to touch
the sun supine, those snapped rays.
Like the men who lifted the lifeless
Marilyn Monroe, they'd been afraid.

Wishing to meet the caravan, to see
the spectacle, there's a young man
riding out into the bleached desert.
Is it worth the emptiness which follows?
He tries to seduce his soul back
with thoughts of beauty – a pared apple,
the sound of the oud, the day-star pinking in,
Ephemeroptera – a short-lived thing.

Daughters of a suicide

The Longcake girls at the top of the lonning,
the back of the barn, the Longcake girls
clustering like the clumps of daffodils
my father and I planted years later
as though sensing this was ground in need
of healing – where they'd stood, frozen limbs,
daisy-print dresses breaking the heart
of my uncle who always remembered seeing them
as he came up the lonning and how he didn't
know what to say (this was all long before
my day); in any case one of the girls
never spoke again. I think it's her
I go round the barn to meet: her mute fury
in the face of grief, nothing further to be said.

Saving the ladybird

Seeing a ladybird curled
in a dried thistle, I put down
my shears. Saving the ladybird –
her back a lovely post-box red,
those arty polka dots – I wasn't exactly
saving the world. But if Donne
could argue as he did for a flea,
is there anything my ladybird – *she* –
can not be?

Tess has a word with Hardy

Tess of the d'Urbervilles, chapter 13

I know you studied hard as a boy,
but if I'm the one only allowed out
in an Old English dusk,
why can't you use that lovely word,
the one which rhymes with musk,
and sort of rhymes with lust?

Why is it when I'm pregnant
you pile up Latinate words?
Dusk isn't dusk, it's 'the constraint
of day neutralised by night',
and my body is 'a flexuous figure',
my walk 'a quiescent glide'.

How thankful I am for a simple line
of pheasants on an alder bough,
a blackbird's slumberous shape
in the rowan tree. Sometimes
I tell you I long to be shelved.
But what about the baby?

Angela

from Keats' 'The Eve of St Agnes'

Without so much as a word,
off they ran, the posh lass I'd nursed
and that young lad.

Sickly candied apple, shrinking plums,
a rim of jelly, dainties on the floor,
syrups they'd ruined with cinnamon –

all my life it's been leftovers.
So if you expect a thank you
for the pickings I found in the lovers' room –

Read My Lips.

Six hen pheasants in my garden last Tuesday

Watching from windows – back bedroom, dining room,
kitchen, stairs – following the nervous progress
of the birds from the old blackcurrant patch
to the snowdrop slope, the plum trees, the shade
between the leylandii and the sycamore line
where, it's hard to imagine, in no time
crimson cherry blossom will fall with the grace
and innocence of snow in an upturned paperweight.
I heard no ticking clocks as my winter afternoon
was absorbed by the flock's intent foraging.
Who would have thought age could make time
feather-light? Who would have thought snow
could weigh down a page and never melt?
All my life I've felt hurried, chased and afraid.

In Rainsbarrow Wood

Take the path from Ulpha
to Millbrow when it plays host
to yellow. Then define the colour
of the trees, their bark, a colour
as seasonal as the daffodil,
as peculiar to the end of winter –
an animal grey, startled.

III

Life can only be understood backwards;
but it must be lived forwards.

Complimentary calendar

The stranger at the door, camera
round his neck, said, 'I'm looking
for March.' The men were lambing.
She offered him tea. She'd never thought
of the place as picturesque. Did he say
'It's ordinariness which is best'?
Anyhow, he didn't miss out the washing
on the line, the stack of fallen slates.
He kept Whitey in, and even Whitey's
hen-shaped shadow, and the roots,
the yew tree's, they were there.
And the air, the flowing air
of that ordinary March day she now saw
as one of the best she'd known.
Without her free copy, the sunlight
would never have been downy,
the dozen doves so composed,
and the chimney smoke – wasn't it
the old apple tree being burnt
that morning, the solid of it floating
into the atmosphere in wonder?
April through December she wouldn't allow
the page to be turned, in case
she forgot the lesson she'd learned.

How to make pasche eggs

(for Rebecca)

On Good Friday get your hands
into thorny hedgerows – gorse flower
to texture the ginger-brown
of the onion's hearty dye.

Let the rain fair up,
let washing be blowy on the line.
Hunt for primrose flower, ferns,
daffodil leaves and something untried.

Four is the right number of eggs
to place on their squares of rag.

Make a bed of gorse, position
the garden finds, then wrap
in onion skins, the *sine qua non*
of pasche eggs.

Parcel up with the string you've ratched:
four *bricolage* bundles, four
mummified heads, four *objets*
as disguised as their name.

Then find that veteran pan,
the dishcloth boiler.

If the eggs survive the contests
of Easter day – the downhill trial,
the tabletop battle – like trophies
display them on the dresser.

Be sure to love the ritualistic boiling,
and the tender unwrapping of the rags
with your grandmother by your side,
as though healing a wound.

Fallen apple tree

On your side since Boxing Day,
this cold April, rain welling
in your washing-line wound,

I find you in leaf,
determined to blossom,
to fruit again.

And my body
after thirty years
still bleeding on cue.

Let me count the ways and the times I've walked round Buttermere

The ways – clockwise or anti? Tradition
dictates anti. The times? The times are lost
like Fleetwith Pike in cloud so cloudy it's more
like a representation of itself.
But why the need to count? When here I feel
as ageless as the water, the shore, the tales
illustrating themselves in the spaces between
the trees of Burtness Wood. But Peggy's Bridge,
that cluster of firs in Warnscale Bottom –
they remind me to imagine myself
in a Caspar Friedrich – a parody
of the first time years ago. It's half past
the hour at the too-cheerily-named bridge,
but oils take time and it's hard to get me to budge.

Custodian

(for John)

I charge you with the afterlife of that moment.
Return periodically across your life and see us
(you in your second decade, me my fifth) still paused

at the gate between Snary Beck and Mockerkin How.
See again the white horse on the fell, the light
gilding its tail as the wind flickered.

We'd passed Snary Beck, Cogra Moss
was behind us, and I thought the animal's poise
as beautiful as anything on earth.

But it's *our* pause, the instinctive accord of it, and the light
which must also have been flickering in *our* hair,
I now find (shifting my gaze) more beautiful.

The Old Chancel, Ireby
(for JN)

Once inside, we place our hands
in the piscina, we find where the host
was stored, we read about the glory days
of the Chancel now stranded mid-field.

There are jars of wild flowers in need
of water, but when the door blows open
it isn't rain which the wind brings,
only a reminder that the weather is lord.

It would not surprise, when at last we leave,
to find horses saddled, waiting,
and rivers graced with fords –
for we are more mortal, on the *qui vive*.

Reading the label

The lion is mid-stride, giant-pawed, kingly.
A five-point crown with an orange stripe

floats over his back while his stylish tail
wraps itself round the loops of a letter *B*.

Baracuta of England. Worn from the days
of childbirths, promotions, property, to hobbies,

my Dad's coat has lost six decades
but only three of its fourteen buttons.

The purple lion, embroidered to last
and outlast, swivels his commanding head:

You are not a daughter of empire, he says,
but your father was one of its smartest sons.

The thing itself

On the sands of Alexandria
is it possible that Caesar
pauses in the light,

free of home, of Rome,
feeling as though – at last –
a weight has been lifted?

The Victorian time capsule buried
beneath Cleopatra's Needle
contains a model of the obelisk itself.

Friday night at the Sphinx

His hand on the door
which translates as *Gentlemen*,

he turns and looks back
to see the one-eyed rose seller

making his way through the tables
to where she sits.

On Friday nights years hence
it will preoccupy him –

where it went,
that sweet-smelling feast

of a moment, the simplest
of life's riddles.

The glow

Finding the crab apples, my astonishment
I'd gauge as being on a par with pilgrims
seeing a tear build in the corner
of the Spanish Virgin's powder-blue eye.
Or those Egyptian passers-by, agape,
saying a year's worth of prayers in one day
to the smiling saint on the roof who gave
city air the sheen of a gleaming corniche.

The fellside gardens of aunts always sheltered
a crab apple, jelly made before the clocks
went back. I've a yearning for jars in a line
on my pantry shelf, but time and again
walks yield nothing. It's dusk. The windfalls glow.
This lonning – my Camino de Santiago.

Low Lorton ¼ High Lorton ¼

If we feel a chill each year
on the day we will die,
does the involuntary nod

I perform here – this oblique
junction complicated further
by the church road forking –

signal back to a lost memory?
Did we once turn off the B road
onto this less-than-four-metres-wide road,

and did we pause here, my father,
long after non-existent traffic
had gone past?

I brake, I reverse, I rest
on the wrought-iron seat,
high and low equidistant.

The monkey clock
(i.m. Hilda Benn)

The monkey's eyes go right, go left.
See the sloping flag floor, the range,
Willie Mackereth on his chair, knees to chin.
See George Mackereth, a white cat on his lap,
The World at One at his elbow.

See the bureau, the day's business,
1972's calendar on March.
Here's Hilda Benn with bread and butter,
a teapot in its cosy. Set them down.
The rain that has decided to fall

on that day at that time is falling.
One moment I see you, says the monkey,
one moment I don't. Where is he,
in his Victorian jacket and tie,
where is he and what does he see now?

Eyes right, eyes left at the window –
Dad's coming to collect his daughters,
hear stories of playing slip-slidey
on the chaise longue in the parlour
behind the back parlour, supervised

by china dogs; how one day George
said the monkey straightened his tie.
The stuffed fox, eyes fixed, told no tales.
He longed for the truth of a bracken patch
at dusk, the breathing of wings.

At the fork in the corridor, Mr Fox,
keeping you in his line of vision,
slowing down time as you head towards him,
the flags moulded to rock, a strip of carpet
to the flags, my young hands

to the pot of bramble jelly
I am returning to the pantry:
turn right at the fox, climb three
stone steps, find the preserves
on the far sconce, feel the rock-cold.

Monkey, turn yourself back.
Let 1972 be on the wall,
let cares be in the bureau,
cats be on laps and let the world
be at one. Let the fox leap

in his case, the tails of china dogs
wag in welcome, let the rain say
I'll fall today. Eyes right,
eyes left. One moment
I see you.

A life in geography

Locate Rosley, my first school.
At the road, look right
then left for cars
(and the ghosts of cars).
Cross to the cemetery.

In the Austrian Museum of Applied Arts

I picture a pear tree being felled,
a nearby boy with over-sized pockets
gathering its last fruit,
while the carpenter's tools
sharpen the light.

In the convent, the stool outlived
the remaining trees in the orchard
seven hundred years and counting.

But if a nun could come back
and join me by this exhibit,
'Goodness', she'd say, 'that old thing.
Where's the comb my father gave me,
the doll I kept all my life, the peace
I found, winter descending,
the snow closing in?'

Remanence

n. Magnetisation remaining after removal
of source of excitation

At shouting distance
from the farm
the trembling begins –

the coat-hanger meeting
the air's memory of a well.
I hear a bucket descend,

see homebound footprints
sinking deeper into air
which has a will –

not to let anything go
from this world, this well
we drink from word by word.

Literacy lesson
Wuthering Heights, Chapter 32

We only learn how life is being lived on that day
at the two houses, thanks to a cart of oats,
newly reaped oats, which happened to pass
as an observant hostler refreshed Lockwood's horse.

So is it good news or bad for the two houses
that the very greenness of the oats
prompted the hostler to put down his pail,
tut-tut and exclaim against Gimmerton folk

late again with their harvest – good news or bad
that dreamy Lockwood woke up to where he was?
If close to Gimmerton then close also to the Grange,
a property he rents. Later there'll be a moon,

but with sunlight blowing on the harebell moors
of September 1802, Lockwood detours to find
the Grange's housekeeper enjoying a meditative pipe
on the horse-steps, and a girl of nine or ten knitting.

Even the peaceful curls of blue smoke from the chimney
are disturbed by the master's change of plan: hot cinders
are raked, fires poked, sheets stretched and scorched,
that quiet courtyard hour in the late sun lost.

Does it make the three-months-dead Heathcliff live again,
the fact that Lockwood, his tenant, walks in the dusk
the stony by-road that branches off to Wuthering Heights
expecting to pay his landlord any monies owing?

It was noon when the cart of oats passed. Moonrise now
as Lockwood nears Wuthering Heights, doors and windows
open to the warmth, the smell of wallflowers and stocks.
Not because of the oats, but because of their greenness

the private idling moments of another housekeeper
are interrupted – Nelly Dean loves on such nights
to sit singing on the threshold, moths the colour
of summer butter fluttering. But in the living room,

Catherine and Hareton, playing teacher and pupil,
turn their page undisturbed. Lockwood must let them roam,
once their work is done, across the moors to the end
the book has longed for and which Hareton can now read.